I Bark, *Therefore* I Am

INNER MONOLOGUES OF THE DOMESTICATED

I Bark, *Therefore* I Am

INNER MONOLOGUES OF THE DOMESTICATED

CHARLOTTE JEAN

THE collective BOOK STUDIO

Incoming!

This smells like it has definitely gone bad. Perfect.

I hope my weirdo owner lets me walk today instead of pushing me around in a baby carriage—again.

Just let them
get a little farther
away from the
picnic basket.
Then we move in.

This is your formal
invitation to
accompany me
to the dog park.

Here,
kitty kitty.

I know he said
we are going to
the park, but that
was definitely the
"we are going to
the vet" voice.

No way I'm losing
to him this time!

The hairless ape
that feeds me is late
again.

Yikes! That Yorkie who wants me to be her boyfriend is on the front lawn again.

If this ball could
throw itself,
then I'd only
need you for
the food thing.

On the bright side, I've recently solved the mystery of what was inside the dinosaur.

I'll give *you* potty training.

This belly is not
going to scratch
itself, buster.

His Netflix binging is really cutting into our "walk time."

No, I don't think it'd be fun for your two-year-old to ride me like a horse, actually.

Finally!
A tree that no other
dog has ever peed on!

And for my next magic trick, I shall make this kitten disappear.

Next time I see
the little girl coming
with the clippies
and hair ties, I'm
making a run for it.

I honestly can't see
a dang thing.

Best.
Pillow.
Ever.

Please, please
let tonight be
"Burger Night."

If this dumb pony
doesn’t blink soon
I’m so going to lose.

Well, that "taking the temperature thing" was pretty awkward.

Please tell me it's
not the 4th of July
and that those
aren't fireworks.

In exchange for teaching me this very important skill, you get to learn how to properly sniff butts.

You're switching me to dry food?

It’s high time for you to get a life and stop dressing me in these ridiculous outfits.

I've tried them all,
and this brand of
toilet definitely
makes the best
drinking water.

You couldn't come up with a more clever name for me than "Spotty"?

I officially
hate you.

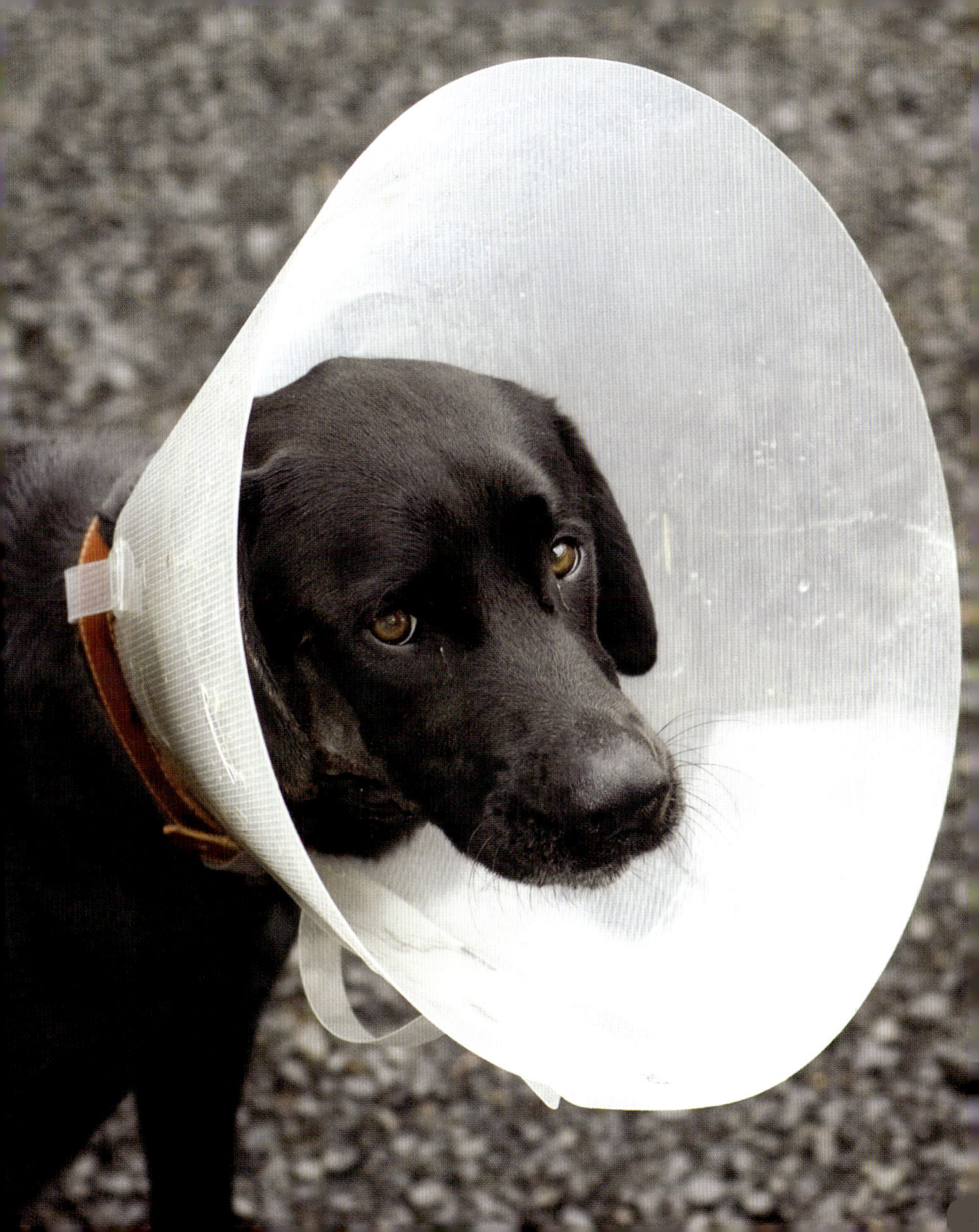

How about *you* sleep
on the floor, and
I just stay right here?

You realize the
second this is over
I'm gonna go roll
on a dead bird.

Know what else is fun? Peeing on the kitchen floor and watching the humans flip out.

Right after this
is my pedi-pedi,
a light lunch,
and then this
“spa day” is a wrap.

If you’re gonna leave me all day to “bring home the bacon,” could you actually bring back some bacon?

There has been a slight setback in my housetraining.

Oh, wait, now I remember you.

I don’t speak cat,
but I am pretty
sure that the hissing
sound means
“please chase me.”

Jackpot!

Yes, I'd love a meatball! That's like combining the two best things in life!

Can you throw this a hundred more times?

The cat and the human can poo inside. But when I do, it's like the world has ended.

Whoever sculpted
you was a genius.

Oh look, a “No dog poop, please” sign. Request denied!

I'm almost ready to run home and break in the new, white couch!

Can you drop something already?

Just a heads up that if we see my dog friends, I'm going to act like I despise you.

Clearly I have no plans to "leave it," so you might as well stop shouting that.

The Dippes

Just keep pretending to look sad until he pulls away, and then let's tear this joint apart!

She is torturing me in a desperate attempt to look cool.

Oh, the new mailman looks delicious!

I need to herd
something
or I'm going to
completely lose it!

It was the cat's idea.

This is humiliating!
Just make a human
baby already!

Ok, you go for it,
and I'll be waiting
right here when
you get back.

Oh, this is comfy up here. Now I know why the cat likes it so much.

This day just keeps getting better and better!

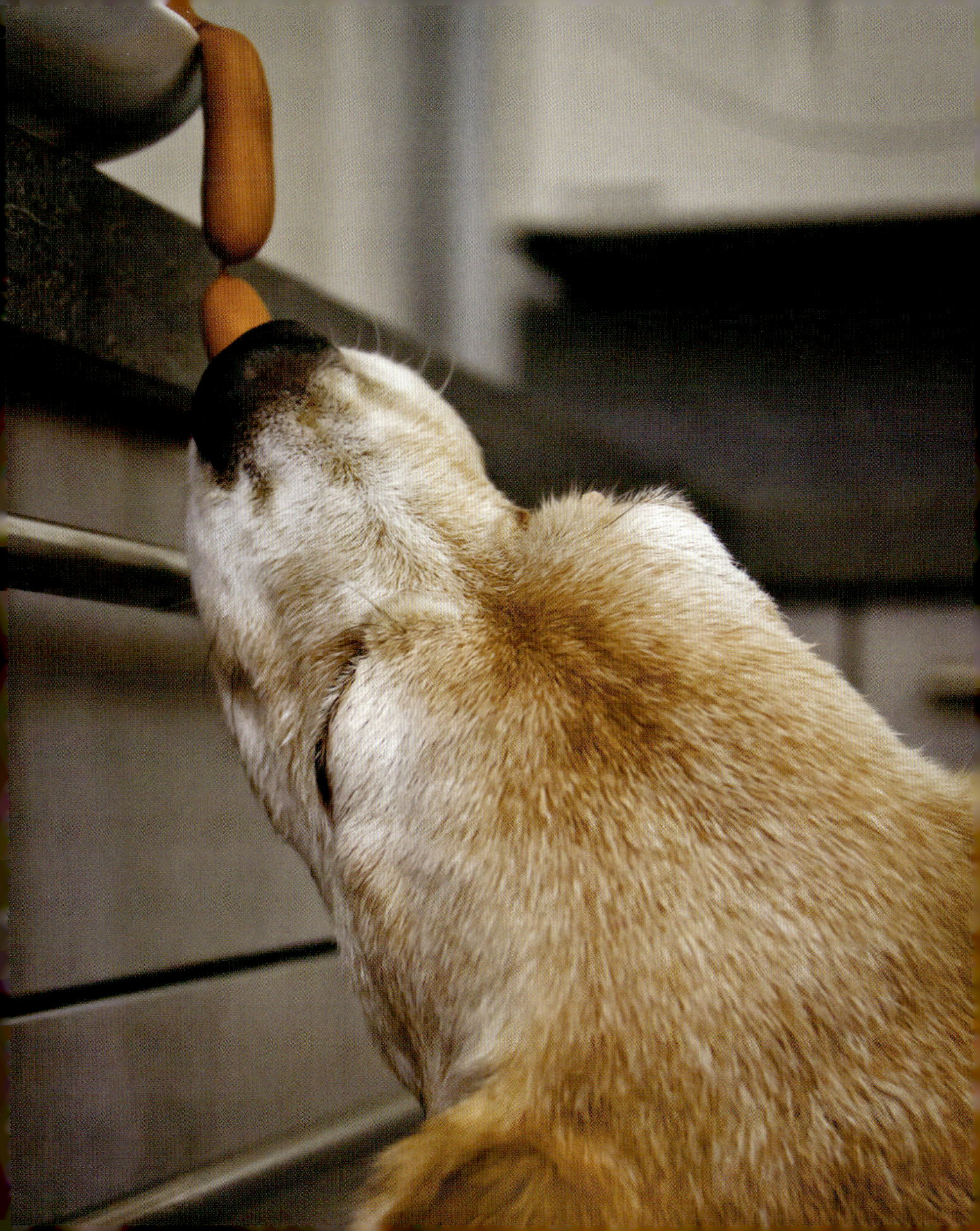

I know that
I'm supposed to be
man's best friend,
but honestly,
I prefer you.

I saw something.
I think it had fins!

Oh my gosh, that poop tasted simply scrumptious.

Hooray! Let's post another pointless picture to Facebook so your fake friends can pretend to care.

You were right . . .
This *is* pretty fun!

Your ear wax is just so delicious!

I wanted a “Slip ‘N Slide,” but this will have to do.

Oh man,
you ARE
taller than me!

Library of Congress Catalog-in-Publication data is available.
ISBN 9781685553135
Ebook ISBN 9781685555986
LCCN 2025920708

Printed in China

FSC
www.fsc.org
MIX
Paper | Supporting responsible forestry
FSC® C102842

Cover and interior design by Rachel Lopez Metzger.
All images courtesy of Shutterstock.

1 3 5 7 9 10 8 6 4 2

The Collective Book Studio®
Oakland, California
thecollectivebook.studio